In memory of Francis Sweeney and h

Disclaimer:

The information provided in this fun fact book is intended for entertainment purposes only. While we have made every effort to ensure the accuracy of the information presented, we cannot guarantee that all of the facts are entirely up-to-date, complete, or free from errors. Moreover, the inclusion of a fact in this book does not necessarily mean that it is universally accepted as true or accurate. Readers should use their own discretion and judgment when relying on any information contained in this book. The author and publishers of this book shall not be held liable for any direct or indirect damages arising from the use or misuse of the information contained herein.

Contents:

Animals

Sloths only defecate once a week because their slow metabolism means they need to conserve as much energy as possible.

Polar bears are nearly invisible under infrared photography because their fur doesn't emit heat.

Kangaroos can't walk backwards because their hind legs are much stronger and longer than their forelimbs.

A group of flamingos is called a flamboyance, likely because of their bright pink feathers that create a striking visual effect when they gather in large groups.

Male seahorses are the ones who give birth because they have a brood pouch where the female deposits her eggs for the male to fertilize and carry to term.

A cat's nose pad is ridged with a unique pattern, just like a human fingerprint, making it possible to identify individual cats.

The blue whale is the largest animal ever known to have existed, growing up to 100 feet in length and weighing as much as 200 tons.

Butterflies taste with their feet, using chemoreceptors to detect the presence of nectar or other nutrients.

A group of crows is called a murder, possibly because of their association with death and their tendency to scavenge carrion.

A rhinoceros' horn is made of compacted hair, which is why it can be trimmed or filed down without causing harm to the animal.

A chameleon's tongue is longer than its body, enabling it to capture insects and other prey from a distance.

Owls can rotate their heads 270 degrees in either direction because of their unique cervical vertebrae and other adaptations that enable them to have a wider range of vision.

A bee has five eyes, including two large compound eyes and three smaller ocelli that detect light intensity and polarisation.

Emperor penguins can stay underwater for up to 20 minutes because of their ability to slow their heart rate and redirect blood flow to essential organs.

A group of lions is called a pride, reflecting the social structure of these big cats, which typically live in family groups consisting of multiple females and their offspring, along with one or more males.

A tarantula can live without food for more than two years, because of their slow metabolism and ability to store energy reserves.

A flamingo's legs are actually white, but their knees bend backwards, making it appear as if they have pink legs because of the pigmentation in their feathers.

A giraffe's neck contains only seven vertebrae, just like a humans, but each vertebra can be up to 10 inches long to allow for the animal's long neck.

A bat is the only mammal that can fly, thanks to their unique wing structure that is made up of thin, flexible membranes of skin stretched over elongated fingers.

A group of whales is called a pod, reflecting their social behaviour and tendency to travel together in groups.

An octopus has three hearts, one that pumps blood to the body and two that pump blood to the gills.

Pigs cannot sweat, which is why they wallow in mud to cool off and regulate their body temperature.

A snail can sleep for up to three years because of their slow metabolism and ability to enter a state of dormancy when conditions are unfavourable.

Koalas sleep for up to 20 hours a day, because their eucalyptus diet is low in calories and nutrients, requiring them to conserve energy.

Alligators can live up to 50 years in the wild, and some have been known to live up to 100 years in captivity.

A group of dolphins is called a pod, but when they come together in larger groups it's called a superpod.

An elephant's trunk contains more than 40,000 muscles and can be used for a variety of tasks, including grasping food, drinking water, and even showing affection.

Goats have rectangular pupils, which allow them to have a wider field of vision and better depth perception.

Camels can close their nostrils to keep out sand and dust during sandstorms, and they can also drink up to 30 gallons of water in just 13 minutes.

An ostrich's eye is bigger than its brain, making it the largest eye of any land animal.

Tigers have striped skin, not just striped fur, which means that even if you were to shave a tiger, it would still have stripes.

A group of jellyfish is called a smack, reflecting the impact they can have on humans if they are stung.

African wild dogs are some of the most successful hunters in the animal kingdom, with a success rate of up to 80% compared to other predators like lions and cheetahs.

The arctic fox is the only species of fox that changes its fur colour based on the season, with a brown coat in the summer and a white coat in the winter.

Sharks have been around for more than 400 million years, predating dinosaurs by about 200 million years.

Seahorses are monogamous and will stay with the same partner for their entire lives, performing elaborate courtship dances to reinforce their bond.

Gorillas have unique nose prints, just like cats and humans, which can be used to identify individuals.

A group of meerkats is called a mob, reflecting their social structure and cooperative behaviour.

African elephants can communicate with each other over long distances using infrasonic sounds that are too low for humans to hear.

Penguins have a gland above their eyes that filters salt from their bloodstream, allowing them to survive on a diet of mostly saltwater fish.

Komodo dragons have a venomous bite that can take down prey much larger than themselves, and they have been known to attack and kill humans.

Whales have a complex social structure and are known to have their own unique dialects of whale songs, which they use to communicate with each other.

Male elephants go through a musth period, during which their testosterone levels increase dramatically, and they become more aggressive and sexually active.

Golden lion tamarins have long, flexible fingers that they use to extract insects and other small prey from tree bark, and they are known for their acrobatic abilities.

An adult male lion's roar can be heard up to five miles away, making it one of the loudest sounds in the animal kingdom.

The pangolin is the only mammal with scales, which it uses for protection against predators, and it's also the most trafficked mammal in the world due to demand for its meat and scales in traditional medicine.

Science & Technology

The first computer mouse was invented in 1963 by Douglas Engelbart, who was trying to find a more intuitive way for people to interact with computers.

The human body produces enough heat in 30 minutes to boil a half gallon of water, demonstrating the remarkable amount of energy produced by our metabolism.

In 1995, the first successful exoplanet orbiting a sun-like star was discovered, opening up new frontiers for the search for life beyond our solar system.

The first solar cell was invented in 1883 by Charles Fritts, who used a layer of selenium to convert light into electricity.

A teaspoon of a neutron star would weigh about 6 billion tons, demonstrating the extreme density and gravitational force of these celestial objects.

The first digital camera was invented in 1975 by Steve Sasson, who created a 0.01-megapixel camera using a CCD sensor and a cassette tape to store the images.

The term "robot" comes from the Czech word "robota," which means forced labour, reflecting the original purpose of these machines as labour-saving devices.

The human eye can distinguish about 10 million different colours, thanks to the three types of colour receptors in the retina.

The first laser was invented in 1960 by Theodore Maiman, who used a ruby crystal to amplify light and produce a focused beam.

In 2012, scientists discovered the Higgs boson particle, which helps explain why particles have mass and is a major milestone in the study of particle physics.

The first website was launched in 1991 by Tim Berners-Lee, who created a way to share information on the internet using HTML and other web technologies.

A computer virus is named after biological viruses because of their ability to replicate and spread through computer systems.

In 2018, a team of scientists used CRISPR-Cas9 gene editing to create the first genetically modified babies, sparking ethical debates about the use of this technology.

The speed of light is approximately 186,282 miles per second, which is the fastest possible speed that anything can travel in the universe.

The first successful heart transplant was performed in 1967 by Dr. Christiaan Barnard, who transplanted a heart from a brain-dead donor into a patient with heart failure.

In 1998, the first module of the International Space Station was launched, marking the beginning of an ongoing international effort to explore space and conduct scientific research.

The human brain contains about 100 billion neurons, each of which can make thousands of connections with other neurons to form complex neural networks.

The first electric battery was invented in 1800 by Alessandro Volta, who used a series of zinc and copper disks separated by moistened cardboard to produce a steady flow of electricity.

In 2012, scientists announced the discovery of the "God particle," another name for the Higgs boson, which helps explain the origin of mass in the universe.

The first successful flight of the Wright brothers' airplane in 1903 lasted just 12 seconds and covered a distance of only 120 feet, but it marked a major breakthrough in aviation history.

In 1957, the Soviet Union launched the first artificial satellite, Sputnik 1, into orbit, marking the beginning of the space age.

The periodic table, which lists all known elements in order of their atomic number and properties, was first developed in 1869 by Dmitri Mendeleev.

The first 3D printer was created in 1984 by Chuck Hull, who used a technique called stereolithography to print a small plastic cup. 3D printing has since advanced to the point where it can print anything from small trinkets to entire houses.

The first commercial video game, Pong, was released in 1972 by Atari. The game consisted of two paddles and a ball that bounced back and forth on the screen, and it became an instant hit. Since then, video games have become a multi-billion-dollar industry with countless games and consoles available on the market.

The concept of nanotechnology was first proposed by physicist Richard Feynman in 1959, who discussed the idea of manipulating individual atoms and molecules to create new materials and structures. Today, nanotechnology is a growing field with applications in everything from medicine to electronics, and scientists continue to make breakthroughs in this area of research.

The human genome, which contains all the genetic information needed to create and maintain a human being, was first sequenced in 2001.

The first successful cloning of a mammal, Dolly the sheep, was accomplished in 1996 by researchers at the Roslin Institute in Scotland.

The world's first artificial heart was implanted in a human in 1982, extending the lives of patients waiting for heart transplants.

Scientists have discovered more than 1.5 million species of fungi, which play an important role in decomposition and nutrient cycling in ecosystems.

The first successful in vitro fertilization (IVF) procedure was performed in 1978, leading to the birth of Louise Brown, the first "test-tube baby.

The world's first commercial spaceport, Spaceport America, opened in New Mexico in 2011, offering commercial spaceflight opportunities to private individuals and companies.

In 2019, researchers at Google's AI lab created a quantum computer that solved a problem in 200 seconds that would have taken the world's fastest supercomputer 10,000 years to solve.

Scientists have estimated that there may be as many as 100 billion planets in our Milky Way galaxy alone, with the potential for many of them to support life.

The first successful cochlear implant, a device that helps deaf people hear, was implanted in a human in 1978.

The first successful organ transplant, a kidney transplant, was performed in 1954 by Dr.Joseph Murray.

In 2015, NASA's New Horizons spacecraft made the first close flyby of Pluto, providing scientists with unprecedented views of this distant dwarf planet.

The first successful vaccination, against smallpox, was developed in the late 18th century by Edward Jenner.

Scientists have discovered more than 4,000 exoplanets, or planets orbiting stars other than our sun, using a variety of techniques including the transit method and radial velocity method.

The first successful magnetic resonance imaging (MRI) scan of the human body was performed in 1977, revolutionizing medical imaging and diagnosis.

The first successful flight of a rocket capable of reaching space was accomplished by German scientist Wernher von Braun and his team in 1944.

In 2017, scientists detected gravitational waves, ripples in the fabric of spacetime, produced by the collision of two neutron stars.

The first successful artificial insemination procedure was performed in 1799 by Italian physician Giovanni Battista Lazzaro Spallanzani.

In 1969, humans first set foot on the moon as part of the Apollo 11 mission, a major milestone in space exploration.

In 2018, a team of Chinese scientists successfully cloned two macaque monkeys using the same technique that produced Dolly the sheep.

Scientists have estimated that there may be as many as 10 million species of insects on Earth, making up the largest group of animals on the planet.

History & World Events

The Great Wall of China is the longest wall in the world, stretching over 13,000 miles. It was originally built in the 7th century BC to protect China from invading nomads.

The assassination of Archduke Franz Ferdinand in 1914 is often considered the spark that ignited World War I. Ferdinand was the heir to the Austro-Hungarian Empire and his death by a Serbian nationalist led to a series of events that eventually led to war.

The American Civil War, which took place from 1861 to 1865, remains the deadliest war in U.S. history, with an estimated 620,000 soldiers killed.

The Declaration of Independence, which announced the thirteen American colonies' separation from Great Britain, was signed on July 4, 1776, and is celebrated as Independence Day in the United States.

The Cuban Missile Crisis in 1962 was a tense standoff between the United States and the Soviet Union over the placement of nuclear missiles in Cuba. The crisis was ultimately resolved peacefully, but it brought the world to the brink of nuclear war.

The Black Death, a deadly pandemic caused by the Yersinia pestis bacterium, swept through Europe in the 14th century, killing an estimated 25 million people, or about one-third of the population.

The Berlin Wall, which separated East and West Berlin from 1961 to 1989, was a symbol of the Cold War and the division between communism and capitalism.

The French Revolution, which took place from 1789 to 1799, was a period of radical social and political upheaval that led to the overthrow of the French monarchy and the establishment of a republic.

The Industrial Revolution, which began in Britain in the 18th century, marked a shift from handcrafted goods to machine-made products and led to significant changes in the way people lived and worked.

The sinking of the Titanic in 1912 remains one of the most famous maritime disasters in history. The ship, which was considered unsinkable, hit an iceberg and sank, killing over 1,500 people.

The fall of the Roman Empire in the 5th century marked the end of the ancient world and the beginning of the Middle Ages in Europe.

The discovery of the Americas by Christopher Columbus in 1492 had a profound impact on world history, leading to European colonization, the transatlantic slave trade, and the formation of new societies and cultures.

The Seven Wonders of the Ancient World, including the Great Pyramid of Giza and the Temple of Artemis at Ephesus, were marvels of engineering and artistry that were considered the most impressive structures of their time.

The Age of Exploration, which began in the 15th century, saw European powers like Portugal, Spain, and England expand their empires and establish trade networks around the world.

The Treaty of Versailles, signed in 1919, officially ended World War I and imposed harsh penalties on Germany, setting the stage for the rise of Adolf Hitler and World War II.

The Holocaust, in which six million Jews were systematically murdered by the Nazis during World War II, remains one of the darkest chapters in human history.

The Renaissance, which took place in Europe from the 14th to the 17th century, was a period of great cultural and artistic growth that saw the emergence of great works of literature, art, and science.

The Battle of Waterloo, fought in 1815, was a decisive battle in which the forces of the French Emperor Napoleon Bonaparte were defeated by a coalition of European armies led by the Duke of Wellington.

The Boston Tea Party, which took place in 1773, was a political protest in which American colonists, angry about British taxation without representation, dumped tea into Boston Harbour.

The invention of the printing press by Johannes Gutenberg in the 15th century revolutionized the way information was disseminated and played a key role in the spread of the Renaissance and the Protestant Reformation.

The Wright Brothers' first successful powered flight in 1903 paved the way for the development of aviation and transformed the way people travelled and communicated.

The formation of the United Nations in 1945 was a response to the devastation of World War II and aimed to promote international cooperation and prevent future conflicts.

The Civil Rights Movement, which took place in the United States from the 1950s to the 1960s, was a struggle for racial equality and justice that led to significant changes in American society and law.

The first successful human heart transplant, performed by South African surgeon Christiaan Barnard in 1967, marked a significant milestone in medical history and opened up new possibilities for organ transplantation.

The Battle of Thermopylae in 480 BCE was a significant battle in which a small force of Greek soldiers, led by King Leonidas I, held off a much larger Persian army for three days.

The signing of the Magna Carta in 1215 was a landmark event in English history that established the principle that everyone, including the king, was subject to the law.

The Opium Wars were a series of conflicts between China and Western powers in the 19th century over the trade of opium. The wars ultimately led to the weakening of the Chinese government and the loss of territory to Western powers.

The Scramble for Africa, which took place in the late 19th and early 20th centuries, saw European powers divide and colonize the African continent, leading to significant social and economic changes.

The Russian Revolution in 1917 led to the overthrow of the monarchy and the establishment of the Soviet Union, which would become a major world power.

The Spanish Inquisition, which took place from the 15th to the 19th centuries, was a brutal campaign by the Catholic Church to suppress heresy and dissent.

The invention of the steam engine in the late 18th century revolutionized transportation and industry, leading to the growth of cities and the expansion of trade.

The construction of the Panama Canal, which began in 1904, was a massive engineering feat that allowed ships to travel between the Atlantic and Pacific Oceans more easily.

The Battle of Stalingrad, fought from 1942 to 1943, was a major turning point in World War II that saw the Soviet Union defeat Nazi Germany in a gruelling battle for control of the city.

The fall of the Berlin Wall in 1989 marked the end of the Cold War and the reunification of Germany.

The Space Race, which began in the late 1950s, was a competition between the United States and the Soviet Union to explore space and demonstrate technological superiority.

The Arab-Israeli conflict, which has been ongoing since the mid-20th century, has had a significant impact on the Middle East and the world at large.

The 1918 flu pandemic, also known as the Spanish flu, infected an estimated 500 million people worldwide and killed between 50 and 100 million.

The establishment of the European Union in 1993 was a major step towards greater integration and cooperation between European nations.

The invention of the telephone by Alexander Graham Bell in 1876 transformed communication and paved the way for the development of modern telecommunications.

The creation of the World Wide Web by Tim Berners-Lee in 1989 revolutionized the way information is accessed and shared around the world.

The Cold War, which lasted from the late 1940s to the early 1990s, was a period of tension and rivalry between the United States and the Soviet Union that shaped world politics and international relations.

The first successful organ transplant, a kidney transplant, was performed in 1954 by Dr. Joseph Murray.

The American Revolution, which took place from 1765 to 1783, saw the thirteen American colonies break away from British rule and establish a new nation based on democratic principles.

The sinking of the Lusitania in 1915, which was carrying American passengers, played a role in the United States' decision to enter World War I.

Art & Entertainment

The longest movie ever made is called "Modern Times Forever" and has a runtime of 240 hours (10 days).

The world's largest snow maze is located in Canada and covers an area of over 30,000 square feet.

The world's first comic book was published in 1837 in Switzerland.

The famous painting "Mona Lisa" was once stolen in 1911 and wasn't recovered until 1913.

The world's smallest cinema is located in Rome and only has one seat.

The first 3D movie was released in 1922 and was called "The Power of Love".

The world's largest collection of video games is owned by a man in Texas and includes over 20,000 games.

The movie "The Revenant" features a scene where Leonardo DiCaprio eats raw bison liver, which was a real event and not a special effect.

The world's largest drive-in theatre is located in Texas and can hold over 3,000 cars.

The world's first animated feature film was called "Snow White and the Seven Dwarfs" and was released in 1937 by Walt Disney.

The world's smallest violin is a real instrument that measures only a few inches in length.

The first recorded opera was performed in Florence, Italy, in 1598.

The world's largest art museum is the Louvre in Paris and has over 380,000 objects in its collection.

The world's largest crossword puzzle was created in China and has over 20,000 clues.

The highest-grossing film of all time is "Avatar", which made over $2.7 billion at the box office

.

The world's first motion picture camera was invented by Thomas Edison in 1891.

The world's largest jigsaw puzzle has over 551,000 pieces and measures 27 feet by 6 feet.

The famous painting "The Scream" by Edvard Munch was stolen twice in the 1990s and both times was recovered by police.

The world's largest indoor waterpark is located in Germany and covers an area of over 215,000 square feet.

The world's smallest museum is located in New York and is only 3.5 feet wide.

The first video game was invented in 1958 by a physicist named William Higinbotham and was called "Tennis for Two".

The world's largest disco ball was built in Kentucky and measures over 30 feet in diameter.

The world's largest Lego tower was built in London and was over 100 feet tall.

The famous Hollywood sign originally read "Hollywoodland" and was built in 1923 as a real estate advertisement.

The world's largest music festival is the Donauinselfest in Austria and attracts over 3 million visitors every year.

The first music video ever played on MTV was "Video Killed the Radio Star" by The Buggles.

The world's largest movie theatre is the Kinepolis in Madrid, Spain, and can hold over 9,000 people.

The world's largest ice sculpture was built in China and measured over 820 feet in length.

The famous painting "Starry Night" by Vincent van Gogh was painted while he was in an asylum and depicts the view from his window.

The world's largest toy museum is located in Missouri and has over 1 million toys in its collection.

The world's oldest known piece of music notation is a cuneiform tablet from ancient Sumeria dating back to around 2000 BCE.

The highest-grossing Broadway show of all time is "The Lion King", which has made over $8.2 billion worldwide.

The world's largest book is the "Bhutan: A Visual Odyssey Across the Last Himalayan Kingdom", which measures 5 x 7 feet and weighs over 133 pounds.

The world's first feature-length animated film was "El Apóstol", which was released in Argentina in 1917.

The world's oldest known surviving film is "Roundhay Garden Scene", a silent short film made in Leeds, England in 1888.

The largest street art mural in the world is located in Rio de Janeiro, Brazil, and measures over 50,000 square feet.

The first known photograph was taken by Joseph Nicéphore Niépce in France in 1826.

The world's largest poetry festival is the Medellín International Poetry Festival in Colombia, which has been held annually since 1991.

The world's largest sculpture is the Spring Temple Buddha in Henan, China, which stands at over 500 feet tall.

The first comic strip to feature a recurring character was "The Yellow Kid", created by Richard F. Outcault in 1895.

The world's oldest known theatre is the Teatro Olimpico in Vicenza, Italy, which was built in 1585.

The world's largest mural made entirely of recycled materials is located in Mexico City and covers over 70,000 square feet.

The world's first color photograph was taken by James Clerk Maxwell in Scotland in 1861.

The highest-grossing concert tour of all time is U2's "360° Tour", which made over $736 million.

The world's largest puppet is the Javanese giant puppet, which can be up to 30 feet tall and is used in traditional Indonesian performances.

The world's first electronic music festival was the "The Glastonbury Fayre" held in the UK in 1971.

The world's oldest surviving musical instrument is a bone flute dating back over 40,000 years, found in Slovenia.

The world's largest film studio complex is Hengdian World Studios in China, which covers over 7.5 square miles.

The world's first radio broadcast of a live sports event was the 1921 World Series between the New York Giants and New York Yankees.

The world's largest collection of comic books is owned by Bob Bretall in California and includes over 101,000 unique issues.

The world's first known playwright was Aeschylus, who wrote in ancient Greece around 2,500 years ago.

The world's largest virtual reality arcade is VR World NYC in New York City, which features over 50 different VR experiences.

The world's oldest surviving play is "The Persians" by Aeschylus, which was first performed in Athens in 472 BCE.

The world's first modern art museum is the Museum of Modern Art (MoMA) in New York City, which opened in 1929.

Nature & The Environment

Lightning strikes the Earth about 100 times per second. Lightning occurs when there is a build-up of static electricity in the atmosphere that needs to be discharged.

The world's largest waterfall, the Angel Falls in Venezuela, is so tall that the water evaporates before it reaches the bottom.

The Dead Sea, located between Israel and Jordan, is so salty that people can float effortlessly on its surface.

The largest desert in the world, the Sahara Desert in Africa, is almost the same size as the United States.

The largest living organism on Earth is a fungus called Armillaria ostoyae, which covers over 2,200 acres in Oregon.

The tallest sand dune in the world, Duna Federico Kirbus, stands over 1,640 feet tall in Argentina.

The world's largest hot spring, located in Yellowstone National Park, is called the Grand Prismatic Spring and is over 300 feet in diameter.

The tallest waterfall in the world, the Salto Angel Falls in Venezuela, drops from a height of over 3,200 feet.

The highest temperature ever recorded on Earth was in Furnace Creek, California, where it reached 134 degrees Fahrenheit in 1913.

The world's largest salt flat, the Salar de Uyuni in Bolivia, covers an area of over 4,000 square miles and is so flat that it's used to calibrate satellites.

The world's largest sand island, Fraser Island in Australia, is over 75 miles long and is the only place in the world where rainforest grows on sand.

The world's largest flower, the Rafflesia arnoldii, can grow up to three feet in diameter and smells like rotting flesh.

The tallest tree in the world, the Hyperion tree, stands over 379 feet tall in California's Redwood National Park.

The world's largest natural arch, the Landscape Arch in Utah's Arches National Park, is over 290 feet long and only 11 feet thick.

The world's largest impact crater, the Vredefort Dome in South Africa, is estimated to be over 186 miles in diameter.

The world's largest volcanic lake, Lake Toba in Indonesia, is over 1,100 feet deep and covers an area of over 440 square miles.

The world's largest cave chamber, the Sarawak Chamber in Malaysia, is over 2,000 feet long and 1,000 feet wide.

The world's largest waterfall system, the Iguazu Falls on the border between Brazil and Argentina, consists of over 275 separate falls.

The world's largest canyon, the Grand Canyon in Arizona, is over 277 miles long and over a mile deep.

The world's largest delta, the Ganges Delta in Bangladesh, covers an area of over 59,000 square miles and is home to over 130 million people.

The world's largest sinkhole, the Great Blue Hole off the coast of Belize, is over 400 feet deep and 1,000 feet wide.

The world's largest saltwater lake, the Caspian Sea, covers an area of over 143,000 square miles and is shared by five countries.

The world's largest karst formation, the Stone Forest in China, covers an area of over 200 square miles and is made up of limestone pillars.

The world's largest coral reef system, the Great Barrier Reef in Australia, covers an area of over 133,000 square miles and is home to thousands of species of marine life.

The world's largest river, the Amazon River in South America, is over 4,000 miles long and is home to some of the most biodiverse habitats on Earth.

The world's largest tree by volume, the General Sherman tree in California, has a volume of over 52,000 cubic feet and is estimated to be over 2,000 years old.

The world's largest glacier, the Lambert Glacier in Antarctica, is over 250 miles long and over 60 miles wide.

The world's largest salt pan, the Etosha Pan in Namibia, covers an area of over 2,700 square miles and is home to a variety of wildlife.

The world's largest freshwater lake by volume, Lake Baikal in Russia, contains over 20% of the world's freshwater and is over 5,000 feet deep.

The world's largest cave system, the Mammoth Cave in Kentucky, USA, is over 400 miles long and is home to unique cave-dwelling creatures.

The world's largest river delta, the Sundarbans Delta in Bangladesh and India, covers an area of over 10,000 square miles and is home to the endangered Bengal tiger.

The world's largest living thing, the Great Barrier Reef, is so large that it can be seen from space.

The world's largest hot desert, the Sahara Desert, is over 3.6 million square miles and covers much of North Africa.

The world's largest mountain range, the Himalayas, stretches over 1,500 miles and includes the highest peak in the world, Mount Everest.

The world's largest carnivorous plant, the Nepenthes rajah, can grow up to 3 feet tall and can digest small mammals and reptiles.

The world's largest salt mine, the Khewra Salt Mine in Pakistan, is over 300 feet deep and produces over 325,000 tons of salt per year.

The world's largest mangrove forest, the Sundarbans in Bangladesh and India, covers an area of over 3,800 square miles and is home to a variety of rare and endangered species.

The world's largest sand desert, the Rub' al Khali in Saudi Arabia, is over 250,000 square miles and is one of the driest places on Earth.

The world's largest river island, Majuli in India, is over 1200 square miles and is home to a unique culture and ecosystem.

The world's largest cave fish, the Giant Devil Catfish in Southeast Asia, can grow up to 9 feet long and weigh over 600 pounds.

The world's largest geothermal power plant, the Geysers in California, USA, generates over 1,500 megawatts of electricity using natural steam from underground.

The world's largest artificial reef, the USS Oriskany in Florida, USA, is over 900 feet long and is home to a variety of marine life.

The world's largest non-polar desert is the Arabian Desert, covering an area of over 900,000 square miles in the Middle East.

The world's largest man-made forest is in China's Shaanxi Province, covering an area of over 13,000 square miles.

The world's largest volcano, Mauna Loa in Hawaii, is over 13,000 feet tall and has erupted 33 times since its first recorded eruption in 1843.

The world's largest hot desert, the Sahara Desert, has temperatures that can reach up to 136°F (58°C) during the day and drop below freezing at night.

The world's largest sandstone arch, the Rainbow Bridge in Utah, has a span of over 275 feet and is only accessible by boat or a 14-mile hike.

The world's largest cave fish, the Chinese cave fish, can grow up to 12 inches long and have adapted to living in complete darkness.

The world's largest geothermal power plant, the Geysers in California, produces enough energy to power over 725,000 homes.

The world's largest man-made lake, Lake Kariba in Africa, covers an area of over 2,000 square miles and was created by building a dam across the Zambezi River.

The world's largest whirlpool, the Moskstraumen in Norway, can reach speeds of up to 20 miles per hour and is over 4 miles wide.

The world's largest mushroom, a specimen of Armillaria ostoyae found in Oregon, covers over 2,200 acres and is estimated to be over 2,400 years old.

The world's largest artificial reef, the Osborne Reef off the coast of Florida, was created by dumping over 2 million tires into the ocean and has become an environmental disaster.

The world's largest inland delta, the Okavango Delta in Botswana, covers an area of over 6,000 square miles and is home to a diverse array of wildlife.

The world's largest canyon system, the Yarlung Tsangpo Grand Canyon in Tibet, is over 300 miles long and reaches depths of over 17,000 feet.

The world's largest hydroelectric dam, the Three Gorges Dam in China, is over 1.4 miles long and produces enough energy to power over 64 million homes.

The world's largest wetland, the Pantanal in South America, covers an area of over 70,000 square miles and is home to over 4,000 species of plants and animals.

The world's largest sand desert, the Rub' al Khali in the Arabian Peninsula, covers an area of over 250,000 square miles and is also known as the "Empty Quarter."

The world's largest natural gas field, the South Pars/North Dome field in the Persian Gulf, spans an area of over 3,700 square miles and holds an estimated 51 trillion cubic meters of gas.

The world's largest outdoor sculpture, the Spring Temple Buddha in China, stands over 500 feet tall and weighs over 1,000 tons.

The world's largest wind farm, the Gansu Wind Farm in China, has a capacity of over 6,000 megawatts and covers an area of over 14,000 square miles.

The world's largest underground lake, the Dragon's Breath Cave in Namibia, is over 1,300 feet long and contains a pool of water that is 330 feet deep.

Food & Drink

In ancient Egypt, beer was so important that it was used as currency. Workers were often paid in beer, and it was also used to pay taxes.

The world's largest pizza was made in Rome, Italy in 2012. It was 131 feet in diameter and weighed over 51,000 pounds.

The hottest chili pepper in the world is the Carolina Reaper, with an average heat level of 1.6 million Scoville heat units (SHU). That's over 200 times hotter than a jalapeño pepper!

Honey never spoils. Archaeologists have found pots of honey in Egyptian tombs that are thousands of years old and are still edible.

The world's most expensive coffee is made from the feces of a civet cat. The cat eats coffee berries, and the undigested beans are collected, cleaned, and roasted. A pound of this coffee can cost up to $600.

The largest fruit in the world is the jackfruit, which can weigh up to 100 pounds. It's commonly used in South Asian and Southeast Asian cuisine.

The world's oldest known recipe is for beer. It was found on a Sumerian tablet from around 1800 BC.

In the 16th century, it was believed that pineapples could cure everything from infertility to scurvy. They were so rare and expensive that people would rent them out as a center-piece for a party.

The world's largest egg was laid by an ostrich in 2008. It weighed almost 6 pounds and was the equivalent of about 24 chicken eggs.

Pigs can get drunk. In 2010, a pig in England drank 18 cans of beer that had been left out by some campers. The pig got so drunk that it passed out and had to be taken to a veterinary hospital.

The world's largest sushi roll was made in 2012 in Japan. It was over 1,000 feet long and weighed over 1,000 pounds.

Some people are allergic to water. It's called aquagenic urticaria, and it causes hives and a rash when the person comes into contact with water.

The world's oldest bottle of wine is over 1,600 years old. It was found in Germany in the 4th century AD and is still intact.

The world's most expensive hamburger costs $5,000. It's made with Kobe beef, foie gras, truffles, and caviar, and it's served on a gold-dusted bun.

Apples, pears, and plums are all members of the rose family.

The world's most expensive spice is saffron, which can cost up to $10,000 per pound. It's made from the dried stigmas of the saffron crocus flower.

In ancient Rome, it was common to add lead to wine to make it sweeter. This practice led to widespread lead poisoning and may have contributed to the fall of the Roman Empire

.

The world's largest chocolate bar weighed over 12,000 pounds. It was made in Armenia in 2010.

The world's most popular fruit is the tomato. It's technically a fruit, not a vegetable.

The world's most expensive tea is called Da Hong Pao, and it can cost up to $1,200 per pound. It's made from leaves that are grown on a rare tea plant in China.

Astronauts often crave spicy food because when in microgravity environment, the sense of smell is reduced due to changes in fluid distribution in the body. Spicy food can help compensate for this reduction by providing a stronger taste experience.

The world's first recorded restaurant, the "Salle des Mangeurs," opened in Paris in 1765.

The world's largest cabbage weighed over 138 pounds and was grown in Alaska in 2012.

The world's most popular spice is black pepper.

Carrots were originally purple, not orange. Dutch farmers in the 16th century bred them to be orange in honour of the House of Orange, a Dutch royal family.

The world's most popular spice blend is curry powder, which originated in India.

In Japan, it is customary to say "Itadakimasu" before a meal, which roughly translates to "I humbly receive." It is a way of expressing gratitude for the food and those who prepared it.

The world's oldest known chocolate bar is from the early 1900s and is on display at the Cadbury Chocolate Factory in the UK.

Most wasabi served in restaurants is actually a mixture of horseradish, mustard, and green food colouring. Real wasabi is very expensive and difficult to grow.

There are more than 1,000 types of bananas in the world, but the most commonly eaten variety is the Cavendish.

The world's most popular herb is parsley.

Tea is the most commonly consumed beverage in the world after water.

The world's most expensive whiskey is The Macallan 1946, which sold for $460,000 in 2019.

The world's most expensive fruit is the Japanese Yubari melon, which can sell for up to $45,000 per pair.

Most wasabi served in restaurants is actually a mixture of horseradish, mustard, and green food colouring. Real wasabi is very expensive and difficult to grow.

The world's most popular spice blend is curry powder, which originated in India.

Health & Medicine

In ancient Greece, doctors used spider webs to make bandages for their patients. They believed that the silk in the webs had medicinal properties.

There is a condition called "Foreign Accent Syndrome" where a person's accent can change after a traumatic brain injury or stroke. The person may start speaking with a completely different accent without realising it.

The average person sheds about 40 pounds of skin in their lifetime. Most of this skin is shed while we sleep.

The longest recorded sneezing fit lasted for 978 days. This was the case of a man named Donal MacGowan who sneezed an average of once every minute and a half.

The world's smallest bone is in the ear. It's called the stapes bone and is about the size of a grain of rice.

Hiccups can be caused by a variety of factors, including eating too quickly, drinking carbonated beverages, and excitement or stress. They are involuntary contractions of the diaphragm muscle that can be annoying, but usually harmless.

There is a rare condition called "Auto-Brewery Syndrome" where the body produces alcohol in the gut after eating carbohydrates. This can lead to a person getting drunk without consuming any alcohol.

The world's largest kidney stone ever recorded weighed over 1.1 kilograms (2.4 pounds). It was removed from a man in Hungary in 2009.

The human nose can detect over 1 trillion different scents. This makes it one of the most sensitive and complex organs in the body.

A person's fingerprints are unique, but so is their tongue print. In fact, some security systems are using tongue prints as a form of identification.

There is a rare genetic condition called "Hypertrichosis" or "Werewolf Syndrome" where a person's body is covered in hair. This condition is caused by a genetic mutation and affects only a few people in the world.

The world's first recorded heart surgery was performed in ancient Egypt around 3,500 years ago. The surgeon used a bronze surgical tool to make an incision in the patient's chest and repair their heart.

The human body can survive for weeks without food, but only a few days without water. This is because water is essential for many of the body's vital functions, including regulating body temperature and removing waste.

The world's oldest known prescription is over 4,000 years old and was written in Sumerian. The prescription was for a type of pain relief that included beer, which was used as an anaesthetic.

There is a condition called "Exploding Head Syndrome" where a person hears loud, imaginary noises in their head, such as explosions or gunshots. This condition can be frightening but is not usually harmful.

Some people have a condition called "Synesthesia" where their senses are cross-wired. For example, they may see colours when they hear music or taste flavours when they see certain shapes.

The smallest muscle in the human body is called the stapedius muscle and is located in the ear. It measures only a few millimeters in length.

The ancient Greeks used to believe that a person's breath was closely linked to their health. They believed that bad breath could be a sign of illness and that sweet-smelling breath was a sign of good health.

The world's first vaccine was developed in 1796 by Edward Jenner to protect against smallpox. Jenner noticed that milkmaids who had contracted cowpox seemed to be immune to smallpox, so he developed a vaccine using cowpox.

There is a rare condition called "Sleeping Beauty Syndrome" or "Kleine-Levin Syndrome" where a person can sleep for up to 20 hours a day. This condition is characterized by periods of excessive sleepiness and hyperphagia (excessive eating) and can last for days, weeks, or even months.

The human body contains enough fat to make seven bars of soap. This fat is primarily stored in adipose tissue, which serves as a reserve source of energy for the body.

There is a condition called "Capgras Syndrome" where a person believes that someone they know has been replaced by an identical imposter. This condition is often associated with schizophrenia or other psychiatric disorders.

The world's first successful heart transplant was performed in 1967 by South African surgeon Christiaan Barnard. The patient survived for 18 days before succumbing to pneumonia.

.

There is a condition called "Alien Hand Syndrome" where a person's hand acts independently of their own will, sometimes performing actions that are contrary to their intention. This condition is often associated with brain injuries or neurological disorders.

The human eye can distinguish up to 10 million different colours, making it one of the most complex and sophisticated organs in the body.

There is a condition called "Munchausen Syndrome" where a person fakes or exaggerates illness in order to receive medical attention. This condition is often associated with a history of abuse or neglect.

The world's oldest person on record was Jeanne Calment, who lived to the age of 122 years and 164 days. Calment was born in 1875 and lived through both World Wars and the invention of the automobile.

There is a condition called "Cotard's Syndrome" where a person believes that they are dead, or that parts of their body are missing or have been replaced. This condition is often associated with depression or other psychiatric disorders.

The human body contains enough iron to make a 3-inch nail. This iron is primarily found in haemoglobin, the protein in red blood cells that carries oxygen throughout the body.

There is a condition called "Savant Syndrome" where a person with a developmental or intellectual disability demonstrates exceptional abilities in a specific area, such as music, art, or mathematics. This condition is often associated with autism spectrum disorder.

The world's largest kidney transplant chain involved 60 surgeries and took place over four months in 2012.

The world's first successful hand transplant surgery was performed in 1998 in Lyon, France.

The human body has enough carbon in it to fill about nine thousand pencils.

The shortest recorded pregnancy that resulted in a live birth was 22 weeks and 6 days.

The first recorded caesarean section was performed on Queen Louise of Prussia in 1817.

Approximately one-third of the world's population is infected with tuberculosis, a bacterial disease that primarily affects the lungs.

The world's first successful artificial heart transplant was performed in 1982 by Dr. William DeVries in Louisville, Kentucky.

Human hair grows at a rate of about 0.5 inches per month.

The world's first successful face transplant surgery was performed in France in 2005.

The human body has enough potassium in it to fire a toy cannon.

The world's first documented case of HIV/AIDS was in a man from the Democratic Republic of Congo in 1959.

The average person has about 100,000 hairs on their head.

The world's first successful penile transplant surgery was performed in South Africa in 2014.

The human heart beats approximately 100,000 times per day.

The world's first successful cornea transplant was performed in 1905.

The human brain contains approximately 100 billion neurons.

The world's first successful lung transplant was performed in 1963 in Jackson, Mississippi.

The average person blinks about 15 times per minute.

The world's first successful pancreas transplant was performed in 1966 in Minneapolis, Minnesota.

The human liver can regenerate itself to its original size within six months of losing up to 75% of its mass.

Sports & Athletics

In basketball, the world's largest basketball was made in Romania and measures 10 feet in diameter.

The record for the fastest marathon while dribbling a basketball is held by Zach Prescott of the United States, who completed a marathon in 4 hours and 13 minutes.

The world's oldest soccer ball was found in the roof of Stirling Castle in Scotland and dates back to the 16th century.

The longest golf hole in the world is the seventh hole at the Sano Course in Japan, which measures 964 yards.

In 2008, Jamaican sprinter Usain Bolt set the world record for the 100-meter dash with a time of 9.58 seconds.

The sport of curling was originally played on frozen ponds in Scotland in the 16th century.

The world's first indoor ice rink was built in London in 1876.

The highest-altitude football game ever played was between two teams in Nepal, at an altitude of 18,800 feet above sea level.

In 2016, the Chicago Cubs won their first World Series title in 108 years.

The first Olympic Games were held in ancient Greece in 776 BC.

The longest game in Major League Baseball history was played between the Chicago White Sox and Milwaukee Brewers in 1984 and lasted 8 hours and 6 minutes.

In cricket, the highest individual score ever made in a single innings is 400 not out, achieved by Brian Lara of the West Indies in 2004.

The first international soccer match was played between Scotland and England in 1872.

The sport of water polo was first played in Scotland in the late 19th century.

The world's first modern Olympic Games were held in Athens, Greece in 1896.

The fastest recorded serve in tennis was made by Sam Groth of Australia in 2012 and measured 163.7 miles per hour.

The largest wave ever surfed was a 78-foot monster surfed by Brazilian surfer Rodrigo Koxa in 2017.

The oldest living Olympic medalist is Hungarian swimmer Agnes Keleti, who won 10 medals between 1948 and 1956 and is still alive at the age of 101.

The first organized game of American football was played between Princeton and Rutgers in 1869.

The first modern Olympic gold medal was won by American athlete James Connolly in the triple jump event at the 1896 Athens Games.

The first-ever basketball game was played in Springfield, Massachusetts, in 1891.

In 2018, the Philadelphia Eagles won their first Super Bowl title in franchise history.

The fastest goal ever scored in a soccer match was scored by Brazilian soccer player Fabinho in just 3.23 seconds.

The world's largest football stadium is the Rungrado 1st of May Stadium in Pyongyang, North Korea, which can hold up to 150,000 people.

The first official modern Olympic mascot was Waldi the Dachshund, who was created for the 1972 Munich Games.

The world's largest cricket stadium is the Motera Stadium in Ahmedabad, India, which can hold up to 110,000 spectators.

The first official world record in athletics was set by William W. Hoyt of the United States, who ran the mile in 4 minutes and 36 seconds in 1865.

The sport of rugby was first played at Rugby School in England in 1823.

The highest score ever achieved in a single game of basketball is 272 points, achieved by a team in a Lebanese basketball league in 2012.

The sport of badminton originated in ancient India and was called "Poona" before it was renamed in the 1800s.

The fastest knockout in boxing history was achieved by Daniel Jimenez of Puerto Rico, who knocked out Harald Geier of Austria in just 17 seconds.

The first modern Olympic Games to feature female athletes were held in Paris in 1900, with women competing in events such as tennis, golf, and croquet.

The sport of hockey originated in Canada in the late 19th century and was first played with a ball before the use of a puck became common.

The longest field goal in NFL history was kicked by Matt Prater of the Denver Broncos, who kicked a 64-yard field goal in 2013.

The sport of volleyball was invented in 1895 by William G. Morgan in Holyoke, Massachusetts.

The first person to run a mile in under four minutes was Roger Bannister of Great Britain, who achieved the feat in 1954.

The world's largest skatepark is the SMP Skatepark in Shanghai, China, which covers an area of 12,000 square meters.

The sport of archery has been included in the Olympic Games since the 1900 Paris Games.

The fastest hat-trick in professional soccer history was scored by Tommy Ross of Scotland, who scored three goals in just 90 seconds in a match in 1964.

The first ever World Cup soccer tournament was held in 1930 in Uruguay, and was won by the host nation.

The highest scoring game in NBA history was played in 1983 between the Detroit Pistons and the Denver Nuggets, with a final score of 186-184 in triple overtime.

The first Wimbledon tennis tournament was held in 1877 and was only open to male players.

The sport of handball was first played in Scandinavia and Germany in the late 19th century and was originally called "indoor football".

The world's first recorded marathon race was held in Greece in 490 BC and was won by a messenger named Pheidippides who ran from Marathon to Athens to deliver news of a military victory.

The highest score ever achieved in a single game of soccer was 149-0, achieved by Stade Olympique de L'emyrne of Madagascar in a match in 2002.

The sport of triathlon was first introduced at the 2000 Sydney Olympics, with athletes competing in swimming, cycling, and running events.

The first ever official international cricket match was played between Canada and the United States in 1844.

The world's largest wrestling competition is the United World Wrestling Championships, which features athletes from over 100 countries competing in freestyle and Greco-Roman wrestling.

Geography & Travel

The Great Barrier Reef is the largest living structure on Earth. It is composed of over 2,900 individual reefs and 900 islands stretching for over 2,300 kilometers off the coast of Australia.

There is a town in Canada called Dildo. It is located in the province of Newfoundland and Labrador.

The Dead Sea, located between Jordan and Israel, is the lowest point on Earth at 429 meters below sea level. Its high salt concentration makes it difficult for swimmers to sink.

The longest place name in the world is Taumatawhakatangihangakoauauotamateaturipukakapikimaungahoro nukupokaiwhenuakitanatahu. It is a hill located in New Zealand and means "The summit where Tamatea, the man with the big knees, the climber of mountains, the land-swallower who travelled about, played his nose flute to his loved one."

The largest sand island in the world is Fraser Island, located off the coast of Queensland, Australia. It is over 120 kilometers long and is home to a variety of unique flora and fauna.

The city of Istanbul, Turkey is the only city in the world that sits on two continents - Europe and Asia.

The deepest post-box in the world is located in Susami Bay, Japan. It is over 10 meters underwater and is used by divers to post their letters.

The only land on Earth not owned by any country is a small area in Antarctica called Marie Byrd Land.

The world's largest landlocked country is Kazakhstan. It is roughly the size of Western Europe and is bordered by Russia, China, Kyrgyzstan, Uzbekistan, and Turkmenistan.

The city of Venice, Italy is built on over 100 small islands and has over 400 bridges.

The world's largest pyramid is not in Egypt, but in Mexico. The Great Pyramid of Cholula is a massive ancient structure that covers an area of over four acres.

The largest salt flat in the world is the Salar de Uyuni in Bolivia. It covers over 10,000 square kilometers and is home to unique geological formations and wildlife.

The city of La Paz, Bolivia is the highest capital city in the world, sitting at an altitude of 3,660 meters above sea level.

The world's largest volcano is Mauna Loa in Hawaii. It stands over 13,000 feet above sea level and is over 60 miles long.

The shortest commercial flight in the world is between the Scottish islands of Westray and Papa Westray. The flight is just 1.7 miles long and takes only a few minutes.

The world's largest waterfall system is the Iguazu Falls located on the border between Argentina and Brazil. It consists of over 275 individual waterfalls and is a UNESCO World Heritage site.

The island nation of Palau is home to a lake that is filled with millions of harmless jellyfish. Visitors can swim with these jellyfish, which have lost their ability to sting due to the lack of natural predators.

The world's largest cave system is the Mammoth Cave system in Kentucky, USA. It has over 400 miles of explored passageways.

The only continent without a desert is Europe.

The world's tallest waterfall is Angel Falls, located in Venezuela. It is over 3,200 feet tall.

Mount Everest, located in the Himalayas, is the highest point on Earth, standing at 8,848 meters above sea level.

The Great Wall of China is the longest wall in the world, stretching over 13,000 miles.

The largest city in the world by population is Tokyo, Japan, with over 37 million people.

The Sahara Desert in Africa is the largest hot desert in the world, covering over 3.6 million square miles.

The world's largest cave chamber is in Vietnam's Son Doong Cave, which is over 650 feet high and 500 feet wide.

The city of Petra in Jordan is an ancient city carved into the rock, and it is one of the New Seven Wonders of the World.

The highest waterfall in North America is Yosemite Falls in California, USA, with a height of 2,425 feet.

The world's largest inland sea is the Caspian Sea, which is bordered by Russia, Kazakhstan, Iran, Turkmenistan, and Azerbaijan.

The city of Amsterdam in the Netherlands is built on over 90 islands connected by over 1,000 bridges.

The Grand Canyon in Arizona, USA, is over 277 miles long and up to 18 miles wide.

The world's largest hot spring is the Grand Prismatic Spring in Yellowstone National Park, USA, with a diameter of over 300 feet.

The city of Marrakech in Morocco is home to one of the busiest squares in Africa, Jemaa el-Fnaa, where vendors sell food, clothes, and crafts.

The Galapagos Islands, located off the coast of Ecuador, are home to many unique species of animals, including the Galapagos tortoise, marine iguana, and blue-footed booby.

The world's largest living bird is the ostrich, which can grow up to 9 feet tall and weigh up to 350 pounds.

The city of Cusco in Peru was once the capital of the Inca Empire and is now a UNESCO World Heritage site.

The Great Ocean Road in Australia is a scenic coastal drive that spans over 150 miles and offers breath-taking views of the ocean and cliffs.

The world's largest archipelago is Indonesia, made up of over 17,000 islands.

The city of Quebec in Canada is the only walled city in North America north of Mexico and is a UNESCO World Heritage site.

The world's largest glacier outside of the polar regions is the Fedchenko Glacier in Tajikistan, which is over 43 miles long.

The city of Dubrovnik in Croatia is known as the "Pearl of the Adriatic" and is a popular tourist destination with its historic Old Town and city walls.

Language & Communication

In English, "gullible" is the only word that doesn't appear in the dictionary. This is often used as a joke to trick people into looking it up.

The longest word in the English language is 189,819 letters long and is the chemical name for the largest known protein, "titin". However, it is rarely used and is not included in most dictionaries.

The most common letter in the English language is "e", while the least common is "z".

The word "oxymoron" is an example of itself, as it combines two contradictory terms, "oxy" meaning sharp and "moron" meaning dull.

The shortest complete sentence in the English language is "I am."

The sentence "The quick brown fox jumps over the lazy dog" contains every letter in the English alphabet.

In Hawaiian, there is only one letter for each vowel, and only eight consonants.

The word "set" has more meanings than any other word in the English language, with over 400.

In American Sign Language, the sign for "spaghetti" is the same as the sign for "worm".

The word "nerd" was first coined by Dr. Seuss in his book "If I Ran the Zoo".

The longest word in the German language is "Donaudampfschifffahrtselektrizitätenhauptbetriebswerkbauunterbeamtengesellschaft", which translates to "Association for Subordinate Officials of the Head Office Management of the Danube Steamboat Electrical Services".

In Chinese, the same word can have many different meanings depending on the tone in which it is spoken. For example, the word "ma" can mean "mother", "horse", "hemp" or "scold" depending on the tone.

The word "meme" was coined by Richard Dawkins in his 1976 book "The Selfish Gene", to describe an idea or behaviour that spreads from person to person within a culture.

The Cherokee language is the only Native American language to have its own writing system, created by Sequoyah in the early 19th century.

The word "ampersand" is a contraction of the phrase "and per se and", meaning "and by itself".

In Old English, the word "girl" was used to refer to both sexes, while "boy" referred specifically to a young male.

The word "queue" is the only word in the English language that is still pronounced the same way when the last four letters are removed.

The word "gymnasium" comes from the Greek word "gymnos", meaning "naked". In ancient Greece, athletes would train and compete in the nude.

The Hawaiian language has only 13 letters, and every word ends in a vowel.

In French, the word "croissant" means "crescent", which is the shape of the pastry.

The word "OK" is the most widely recognized and used word in the world and is understood in almost every language.

In Esperanto, every letter is pronounced the same way, and words are spelled exactly as they sound.

The word "onomatopoeia" refers to words that imitate the sound they represent, such as "buzz", "hiss", and "boom".

In Japanese, hiragana and katakana are syllabic writing systems, while kanji is based on Chinese characters and consists of ideographic characters that represent words or concepts.

The word "nerd" was first coined by Dr. Seuss in his book "If I Ran the Zoo".

In Chinese, the same word can have many different meanings depending on the tone in which it is spoken. For example, the word "ma" can mean "mother", "horse", "hemp" or "scold" depending on the tone.

The word "meme" was coined by Richard Dawkins in his 1976 book "The Selfish Gene", to describe an idea or behaviour that spreads from person to person within a culture.

The Cherokee language is the only Native American language to have its own writing system, created by Sequoyah in the early 19th century.

The word "ampersand" is a contraction of the phrase "and per se and", meaning "and by itself".

In Old English, the word "girl" was used to refer to both sexes, while "boy" referred specifically to a young male.

The word "queue" is the only word in the English language that is still pronounced the same way when the last four letters are removed.

The word "gymnasium" comes from the Greek word "gymnos", meaning "naked". In ancient Greece, athletes would train and compete in the nude.

The Hawaiian language has only 13 letters, and every word ends in a vowel.

In French, the word "croissant" means "crescent", which is the shape of the pastry.

The word "OK" is the most widely recognized and used word in the world and is understood in almost every language.

In Esperanto, every letter is pronounced the same way, and words are spelled exactly as they sound.

The word "onomatopoeia" refers to words that imitate the sound they represent, such as "buzz", "hiss", and "boom".

In Japanese, hiragana and katakana are syllabic writing systems, while kanji is based on Chinese characters and consists of ideographic characters that represent words or concepts.

The International Phonetic Alphabet is a system of phonetic notation based on the Latin alphabet, designed to represent the sounds of spoken language.

In Russian, there are no articles (a, an, the), which can make it difficult for Russian speakers to use them correctly in English.

English is the official language of the skies, and all pilots must be able to speak it fluently regardless of their native language.

There are approximately 6,500 spoken languages in the world, but over half of the world's population speaks just 23 of them.

In some African languages, such as Xhosa, a single word can contain an entire sentence or phrase within it, making them very difficult to translate.

In linguistics, the study of the relationship between words and their meanings is called semantics.

Mythology & Folklore

In Norse mythology, the god Thor once dressed up as a bride to retrieve his stolen hammer. This myth is often celebrated in Nordic weddings.

In Greek mythology, there is a creature called the Chimaera, which had the body of a lion, the head of a goat, and the tail of a serpent.

The ancient Greeks believed that the god Apollo was responsible for the daily rising and setting of the sun.

The Phoenix is a mythical bird that is said to be reborn from its own ashes. This creature is often associated with resurrection and immortality.

The ancient Egyptians believed that the god Anubis was responsible for leading the souls of the dead into the afterlife.

The myth of the Minotaur, a creature with the body of a man and the head of a bull, is said to have inspired the creation of the labyrinth, a maze-like structure with many twists and turns.

In Japanese folklore, there is a creature called the Kappa, a mischievous water spirit that is said to lure people into the water and drown them.

The ancient Greeks believed that the god Hermes was responsible for protecting travellers and merchants.

The myth of the Medusa, a woman with snakes for hair, is said to have inspired the creation of the Gorgon, a type of protective shield that is often decorated with images of snakes.

In Hindu mythology, the god Ganesh is often depicted with the head of an elephant. This is said to represent the god's wisdom and knowledge.

In Norse mythology, the god Odin had two ravens named Hugin and Munin, who would fly around the world and bring back news to Odin.

The ancient Greeks believed that the god Dionysus was responsible for wine, fertility, and ecstasy.

The myth of the Sphinx, a creature with the body of a lion and the head of a human, is said to have inspired the creation of the sphinx, a type of protective statue that is often found in front of temples and other important buildings.

In Chinese mythology, the dragon is often depicted as a symbol of power, strength, and good luck.

The ancient Egyptians believed that the god Ra was responsible for the sun, and that he would sail his sun boat across the sky each day.

The myth of the Cyclops, a creature with a single eye in the center of its forehead, is said to have inspired the creation of the cyclopean style of architecture, which features massive stone blocks that were believed to have been moved by giants.

In Hindu mythology, the god Vishnu is often depicted with four arms, each holding a different symbol of his power.

The ancient Greeks believed that the god Poseidon was responsible for the sea, and that he would sometimes use his trident to create storms and earthquakes.

The myth of the Harpy, a creature with the body of a bird and the head of a woman, is said to have inspired the creation of the term "harpie" to describe an annoying or nagging woman.

In Norse mythology, the god Loki was known for his mischief and trickery and was often blamed for causing trouble and chaos.

The ancient Egyptians believed that the god Osiris was responsible for the afterlife and that he would judge the souls of the dead and determine their fate.

The myth of the Hydra, a creature with many heads that grew back whenever one was cut off, is said to have inspired the creation of the Hydra constellation, which can be seen in the night sky.

In Chinese mythology, the Phoenix is often depicted as a symbol of peace and prosperity.

In Greek mythology, the Fates were three goddesses who controlled the destiny of every person. Clotho spun the thread of life, Lachesis measured its length, and Atropos cut it at the end of a person's life.

In Norse mythology, the Valkyries were warrior maidens who selected those who would die in battle and bring them to Valhalla, a hall in Asgard where the brave warriors would feast and fight until Ragnarok.

The legend of King Arthur and the Knights of the Round Table is a well-known tale in British folklore. According to the legend, King Arthur led a group of knights who were known for their chivalry and bravery, and they searched for the Holy Grail.

In Japanese folklore, the Tanuki is a mischievous raccoon dog that is known for its shape-shifting abilities and love of sake.

In Greek mythology, the Titan Prometheus was punished for stealing fire from the gods and giving it to humans. Zeus had him chained to a rock, where an eagle would eat his liver every day, only for it to grow back overnight.

In Norse mythology, the goddess Freya was associated with love, beauty, and fertility. She was also known for her magical necklace, Brísingamen.

The legend of Robin Hood is a well-known tale in English folklore. Robin Hood was a skilled archer who robbed from the rich to give to the poor.

In Hindu mythology, the god Shiva is often depicted with a third eye, which represents his wisdom and ability to see beyond the physical world.

In Greek mythology, the Nemean Lion was a fierce creature with impenetrable skin that was killed by Hercules as one of his twelve labors.

In Native American folklore, the Wendigo is a cannibalistic creature that is said to haunt the forests of the Great Lakes region.

In Norse mythology, the god Freyr was associated with fertility and was often depicted holding a phallic symbol.

In Greek mythology, the Gorgons were three sisters with snakes for hair. One of them, Medusa, could turn people to stone with her gaze.

In Egyptian mythology, the god Thoth was associated with wisdom, writing, and magic. He was often depicted with the head of an ibis bird.

In Celtic folklore, the Banshee is a spirit that is said to wail when someone is about to die.

In Japanese folklore, the Tengu is a humanoid bird creature that is known for its martial arts skills and love of mischief.

In Hindu mythology, the goddess Kali is often depicted with black skin and multiple arms, and is associated with death, destruction, and creation.

In Greek mythology, the Chimera was a fearsome creature with the body of a lion, the head of a goat, and the tail of a serpent.

In Norse mythology, the goddess Hel was responsible for ruling over the realm of the dead. She was said to be half-dead and half-alive, and was often depicted as having a pale face and a gloomy demeanour.

In Egyptian mythology, the god Sobek was associated with the Nile river and was often depicted as a crocodile or a man with a crocodile head.

In Greek mythology, the Harpies were winged creatures with the body of a bird and the head of a woman. They were known for stealing food and causing chaos.

Religion & Spirituality

In the ancient religion of Zoroastrianism, dogs were believed to be sacred and were often buried with their owners.

The Church of the Flying Spaghetti Monster is a satirical religion that was created in 2005 as a protest against the teaching of creationism in schools.

In some Buddhist traditions, it is believed that there is a realm of existence where beings have a single giant eye that covers their entire body.

In some Native American cultures, the dream catcher is believed to protect the sleeping individual from bad dreams and negative energy.

The Great Mosque of Djenne in Mali is made entirely of mud bricks and is the largest mud-brick building in the world.

In the Hare Krishna religion, the mantra "Hare Krishna" is considered the most powerful tool for achieving enlightenment and liberation from the cycle of birth and death.

The goddess Kali in Hindu mythology is often depicted with a necklace of human heads and a skirt made of human arms.

The Japanese Shinto religion believes that everything in nature, from rocks to trees, has a spirit, or kami, which must be honoured and respected.

The religious leader Rael, founder of the Raelian movement, claims to have been contacted by extra-terrestrial beings who revealed the secrets of the universe to him.

In some African traditional religions, twins are considered to have magical powers and are believed to bring good luck.

The Church of Euthanasia is a controversial religion that promotes population control and advocates for suicide, abortion, and cannibalism.

In ancient Egyptian religion, the god Horus was believed to have the power to bring the dead back to life.

The Church of Scientology was founded by science fiction writer L. Ron Hubbard and teaches that humans are immortal beings with unlimited potential.

In some Native American cultures, the rite of passage for young men involves a vision quest, where they spend time alone in nature to seek spiritual guidance.

The Greek god Apollo was known as the god of music, prophecy, and healing. He was often depicted with a lyre and a snake, which were symbols ofhis powers.

In some African traditional religions, the practice of ancestor worship is believed to connect the living with their deceased loved ones and give them guidance and protection.

The Bahá'í Faith, founded in 19th century Persia, teaches the unity of all religions and the essential oneness of humanity.

The Norse god Loki is known as the trickster god and is often portrayed as a mischievous troublemaker who causes chaos and confusion.

The Native American Hopi tribe believes in a prophesied "Fifth World" where the Earth will be destroyed and reborn, leading to a new era of peace and harmony.

The Church of Satan, founded by Anton LaVey in 1966, is a religion that promotes individualism, self-indulgence, and the rejection of Christian values.

The ancient Egyptian goddess Isis was known as the goddess of fertility and motherhood. She was often depicted with a throne on her head and a solar disk between her horns.

In the Baha'i Faith, the number 19 is considered sacred and appears frequently in religious texts and rituals.

The Aztecs believed that the god Quetzalcoatl created humans by dipping bones in his own blood and scattering them on the ground.

The mystical Jewish tradition of Kabbalah teaches that the Torah contains hidden meanings and that the study of its secrets can lead to spiritual enlightenment.

In Sikhism, the holy book is called the Guru Granth Sahib and is considered the living guru. It contains the teachings and wisdom of the 10 Sikh gurus and other saints and scholars.

The Wiccan religion is a modern pagan religion that emphasizes reverence for nature and the cycles of the seasons. It is often associated with witchcraft and magic.

The Hindu god Ganesha is often depicted with an elephant head and is considered the remover of obstacles and the god of wisdom and beginnings.

The Sufi tradition within Islam emphasizes a personal, mystical relationship with God and includes practices such as meditation, chanting, and dancing.

The Roman god Jupiter was the king of the gods and was associated with lightning and thunder. He was also considered the protector of the Roman state.

In the Taoist tradition, the concept of yin and yang represents the balance and interdependence of opposite forces, such as light and dark or hot and cold.

The ancient Greek goddess Athena was the goddess of wisdom, warfare, and crafts. She was often depicted wearing a helmet and carrying a shield and spear.

The Rastafarian religion, which originated in Jamaica, is based on a belief in the divinity of Haile Selassie I, the former emperor of Ethiopia.

In the Jain religion, monks and nuns practice strict nonviolence and take great care not to harm any living beings, even insects or plants.

The Aztecs believed in a pantheon of gods and goddesses, including the sun god Huitzilopochtli and the goddess of fertility Xochiquetzal.

The Muslim holy month of Ramadan is a time of fasting, prayer, and reflection, during which believers abstain from food, drink, and other pleasures from sunrise to sunset.

The ancient Greek god Dionysus was the god of wine, fertility, and ecstasy. He was often associated with wild parties and celebrations.

In the Rastafarian religion, the use of marijuana is considered a sacrament and a way to connect with the divine.

The Christian holiday of Easter is celebrated to commemorate the resurrection of Jesus Christ from the dead.

The goddess Athena in Greek mythology was born fully grown and armoured from the head of her father Zeus.

The Sikh religion prohibits the consumption of meat from animals that have been slaughtered in a ritualistic or non-humane manner.

In the Yoruba religion of West Africa, there is a pantheon of gods and goddesses known as the Orishas, each of whom has a distinct personality and domain of influence.

The Taoist philosopher Lao Tzu is believed to have written the Tao Te Ching, a foundational text of Taoism that emphasizes the wisdom of living in harmony with nature.

The Christian Bible is divided into two main sections: the Old Testament, which contains the Hebrew scriptures, and the New Testament, which tells the story of Jesus Christ and the early Christian church.

Fashion & Style

High heels were originally worn by men in the 1600s as a way to make them appear taller and more powerful.

In the 1800s, women in Europe would wear dresses made of feathers, often from birds of paradise, as a status symbol.

The iconic "little black dress" was made popular by Coco Chanel in the 1920s, who believed that black was the perfect colour for any occasion.

Men's neckties were originally worn by Croatian soldiers in the 17th century as part of their uniform and were then adopted by French soldiers in the 18th century.

The practice of wearing makeup can be traced back to ancient Egypt, where both men and women would use it for aesthetic and religious reasons.

In the 1960s, miniskirts were a controversial fashion trend that caused outrage among conservative groups who felt they were too revealing.

During the Renaissance, it was fashionable for women to pluck their hairlines to create a high forehead, which was seen as a sign of intelligence.

The iconic white dress worn by Marilyn Monroe in the movie "The Seven Year Itch" was sold at auction in 2011 for over $4.5 million.

Platform shoes were popular in the 1970s, and some were so high that they required a cane to walk in.

The red-soled shoes made by designer Christian Louboutin have become a status symbol and are often associated with high fashion and luxury.

The traditional Scottish garment, the kilt, was originally worn as a full-length garment, but was shortened to its current length in the 18th century for practicality.

Sunglasses were originally invented in the 12th century by Chinese judges to conceal their facial expressions in court.

In the 18th century, it was fashionable for women to wear tall wigs, which were often adorned with flowers, feathers, and other ornaments.

The iconic trench coat was originally designed as a military garment for soldiers in World War I, but later became a popular fashion item.

The "boater" hat, which is typically made of straw and has a flat top and brim, was originally worn by sailors in the late 19th century.

The term "denim" comes from the French phrase "serge de Nîmes," which refers to the type of fabric that jeans are made from.

In the 1920s, women's fashion saw a major shift as hemlines rose and corsets were abandoned, leading to more comfortable and functional clothing.

The traditional Japanese garment, the kimono, is made from a single bolt of fabric and can be folded and draped in a variety of ways to create different styles.

The "little white dress" became popular in the 1950s, as a simpler and more casual alternative to the little black dress.

The "bikini" was named after the Bikini Atoll in the Pacific, which was the site of nuclear testing in the 1940s.

In the 1980s, "power dressing" became popular, with women wearing suits and shoulder pads to project a more confident and assertive image.

The traditional Indian garment, the sari, is made from a single piece of fabric that can be draped and wrapped in a variety of ways to create different styles.

The iconic "jean jacket" was popularized by Levi Strauss in the 1880s as a durable and practical work garment.

In the 19th century, corsets were so tightly laced that they could cause internal damage, leading to the development of the health corset," which was designed to be less constrictive and more supportive of the back and hips, while still emphasizing the waistline and providing a more natural posture.

The fashion trend of ripped jeans emerged in the 1970s as a symbol of rebellion and counter-culture.

The first fashion magazine, "Gazette du Bon Ton," was published in France in 1912, featuring illustrations of the latest couture designs.

High-waisted pants were popular in the 1940s as a way to conserve fabric during wartime rationing.

Leather jackets became popular in the 1950s, thanks in part to the iconic look of movie rebels like James Dean.

The iconic Birkin bag by Hermès is named after actress and singer Jane Birkin, who complained to the company's CEO about not being able to find a suitable bag for her needs.

The "midi" length, which falls between the knee and ankle, became popular in the 1960s as a more modest alternative to the mini-skirt.

The traditional African garment, the dashiki, has become a symbol of African pride and heritage in the United States since the Civil Rights era.

Flapper fashion in the 1920s featured shorter hemlines, loose-fitting garments, and bold accessories, reflecting a newfound sense of freedom and rebellion among young women.

Bow ties were originally worn by Croatian mercenaries in the 17th century and were later adopted by upper-class gentlemen as a fashion statement.

Animal prints have been a fashion trend since ancient times, with animal skins and furs being used as symbols of wealth and status.

The traditional Middle Eastern garment, the abaya, is a loose-fitting cloak worn over clothing, often in black or other neutral colours.

The punk fashion movement in the 1970s and 80s featured ripped clothing, safety pins, and bold graphics, reflecting a rebellious and anti-establishment attitude.

The "cold shoulder" trend, which features tops and dresses with cut-outs at the shoulders, became popular in the early 2010s.

The traditional Native American garment, the moccasin, has become a popular footwear style in Western fashion, often featuring fringe and beadwork.

The "little red dress" has become a popular alternative to the little black dress, offering a bold and eye-catching pop of colour.

Tie-dye fashion emerged in the 1960s as a symbol of peace, love, and the hippie movement.

The traditional Chinese garment, the qipao or cheongsam, is a form-fitting dress with a high collar and slit skirt, often made from silk or other luxurious fabrics.

Overalls were originally designed as workwear in the 1800s, but later became a popular fashion item, particularly among young people.

The traditional African headwrap, known as a gele or turban, has become a popular fashion accessory in recent years, often featuring bold prints and colours.

Business & Economics

The world's first vending machine was invented in ancient Greece and dispensed holy water in exchange for a coin. Vending machines have come a long way since then and are now used to sell everything from snacks to electronics.

The world's most expensive meat is Wagyu beef from Japan. The cows are fed a special diet and are massaged daily to ensure they produce the highest quality beef. A single steak can cost hundreds of dollars.

The largest employer in the world is the United States Department of Defense, with over 3 million employees.

The first patent ever issued was for a process of making salt. Patents are still an important part of the business world today and are used to protect new inventions and ideas.

The world's oldest company is Kongo Gumi, a construction company in Japan that has been in business for over 1,400 years.

The world's largest shopping mall is the Dubai Mall, which has over 1,200 stores and covers an area of 5.9 million square feet.

The world's first stock exchange was established in Amsterdam in 1602. Today, the stock market is a vital part of the global economy and is used by businesses to raise capital and investors to make money.

The world's largest company by revenue is Walmart, with over $500 billion in annual revenue. Walmart is a retail giant with stores in 27 countries and employs over 2 million people.

The world's smallest country by land area is Vatican City, which is just 0.17 square miles in size. Despite its small size, the Vatican is an important centre of religious and cultural activity.

The world's first credit card was introduced in 1950 by the Diners Club. Today, credit cards are a common way for people to pay for goods and services, and many offer rewards and cash back programs.

The world's largest economy is the United States, with a GDP of over $20 trillion. The U.S. is a major player in the global economy and has a significant impact on economic policy around the world.

The world's first multinational corporation was the Dutch East India Company, which was established in 1602. The company was one of the most powerful and influential organizations in the world for over 200 years.

The world's most valuable brand is Apple, with a brand value of over $200 billion. Apple is known for its innovative products and is a leader in the technology industry.

The world's first automated teller machine (ATM) was installed in London in 1967. ATMs have revolutionized the way people access and manage their money.

The world's largest oil producer is the United States, followed by Saudi Arabia and Russia. Oil is a vital resource for the global economy and is used to power cars, planes, and ships, among other things.

The world's first online shopping transaction took place in 1994, when a man in New Hampshire bought a CD from a website. Today, online shopping is a multi-billion dollar industry and is used by people all over the world.

The world's largest online retailer is Amazon, with over 150 million users and over 2 million sellers. Amazon offers a wide range of products and services, including books, electronics, and streaming video.

The world's first skyscraper was the Home Insurance Building in Chicago, which was completed in 1885. Skyscrapers have become an iconic feature of modern cities and are a symbol of economic progress and growth.

The term "blue chip" comes from the game of poker, where blue chips are traditionally worth the most. In the business world, blue chip companies are those that are well-established, financially stable, and have a reputation for quality.

The term "venture capital" refers to funding provided to startup companies with high growth potential. Venture capitalists often take an equity stake in the company in exchange for their investment.

The world's largest employer in the private sector is Walmart, with over 2 million employees worldwide.

The world's largest producer of gold is China, followed by Australia and Russia.

The first recorded stock market crash occurred in 1637 in Amsterdam, when tulip bulbs were traded at inflated prices and then suddenly collapsed in value.

The term "invisible hand" was coined by economist Adam Smith to describe the self-regulating nature of the market. According to Smith, when individuals act in their own self-interest, the market will automatically adjust to ensure the most efficient allocation of sources.

The United States has the highest number of billionaires in the world, followed by China and India.

The world's largest exporter is China, followed by the United States and Germany.

The concept of "disruptive innovation" was popularized by Harvard professor Clayton Christensen, who argued that new technologies or business models can disrupt established industries and create new markets.

The world's largest container port is Shanghai, China, with a throughput of over 42 million twenty-foot equivalent units (TEUs) per year.

The term "crowdfunding" refers to the practice of raising funds for a project or business venture from a large number of individuals, typically through online platforms.

The largest hedge fund in the world is Bridgewater Associates, with over $140 billion in assets under management.

The term "black swan event" refers to an unexpected and rare event that has a major impact on the economy or financial markets. The COVID-19 pandemic is a recent example of a black swan event.

The world's largest advertising agency is WPP, with over 100,000 employees in 112 countries.

The term "monopoly" refers to a situation in which a single company or group controls the supply of a particular product or service, giving them significant pricing power.

The world's largest food company is Nestle, with over $90 billion in annual revenue.

The concept of "economic moat" refers to a company's ability to maintain a competitive advantage over its rivals, often through factors such as brand recognition, economies of scale, or patents.

The world's largest shipping company is Maersk, with a fleet of over 700 vessels and a presence in more than 100 countries.

The term "bottom line" refers to a company's net income, or the amount of profit that remains after all expenses have been deducted.

The world's largest private equity firm is Blackstone, with over $600 billion in assets under management. Private equity firms invest in and acquire companies with the aim of improving their financial performance and then selling them for a profit.

Politics & Government

In Bhutan, the government uses a Gross National Happiness (GNH) index instead of Gross Domestic Product (GDP) to measure the country's progress.

The smallest republic in the world is Nauru, an island nation in the Pacific Ocean that is only 8.1 square miles.

The United States has the world's longest constitution, with 7 articles and 27 amendments.

In Andorra, a small country located between France and Spain, there are two co-princes who serve as the heads of state: the President of France and the Bishop of Urgell in Catalonia, Spain.

The President of Mexico is limited to a single six-year term in office and cannot run for re-election.

In 2015, New Zealand granted personhood to the Whanganui River, making it the first river in the world to be recognized as a legal person.

North Korea has a government-approved list of 28 hairstyles that its citizens are allowed to have.

The Vatican City, an independent city-state surrounded by Rome, is the smallest country in the world.

In Belgium, voting is compulsory, and citizens who fail to vote can face fines or even imprisonment.

The Prime Minister of the United Kingdom is not required to live in 10 Downing Street, the official residence of the Prime Minister.

In Saudi Arabia, women were not allowed to vote until 2015.

Liechtenstein, a small country located between Switzerland and Austria, is the world's largest exporter of false teeth.

The United States is the only country in the world that does not use the metric system as its official system of measurement.

The President of Iceland is not allowed to own a dog.

The French national anthem, "La Marseillaise," was originally a revolutionary war song and was banned in several European countries for its violent and subversive lyrics.

In Switzerland, all men aged 18-34 are required to perform military service, while women have the option to serve.

In Denmark, all political parties are required to have an equal number of male and female candidates on their electoral lists.

The official language of the European Union is not English, but rather it has 24 official languages.

The flag of Libya is the only national flag in the world to be of a single colour, green.

In Germany, it is illegal to display a Nazi flag or to perform a Nazi salute.

In India, the official language is Hindi, but there are 22 other recognized languages spoken throughout the country.

In Finland, prisoners are allowed to vote in national elections.

The national animal of Scotland is the unicorn.

In the United States, the Presidential motorcade always includes a decoy vehicle.

The official language of the United Nations is English, French, Spanish, Arabic, Chinese, and Russian.

The first country in the world to grant women the right to vote was New Zealand in 1893.

In 2016, the Prime Minister of Iceland resigned after being implicated in the Panama Papers scandal.

The current flag of Japan has been in use since 1870 and is the oldest national flag still in use.

The official language of Malaysia is Malay, but English is widely spoken and is the language of business and commerce.

The United States is the only country to have used nuclear weapons in warfare.

In Israel, it is illegal to import non-kosher meat or to keep a pig as a pet.

Sweden has the world's oldest parliamentary democracy, dating back to 1719.

China has the world's largest standing army, with over 2 million active personnel.

India has the world's largest democracy, with over 900 million eligible voters.

In Canada, the Prime Minister is not directly elected by the people but is appointed by the Governor General, who represents the British monarch.

In South Africa, there are 11 official languages, reflecting the country's diverse cultural heritage.

The President of the Philippines is limited to a single six-year term in office and cannot run for re-election.

In Iran, the Supreme Leader holds ultimate power, and the President serves as a figurehead.

In Australia, voting is compulsory for citizens aged 18 and over, and those who fail to vote can face fines.

In Norway, the government's wealth fund is the largest sovereign wealth fund in the world, with over $1 trillion in assets.

In Thailand, it is illegal to insult the monarchy, and violators can face lengthy prison sentences.

The President of France is elected for a term of five years and can serve a maximum of two consecutive terms.

In Brazil, voting is compulsory for citizens aged 18-70, and those who fail to vote can face restrictions on their ability to access government services.

In Russia, the President is limited to two consecutive terms in office but can run again after a break of at least one term.

In South Korea, the President is limited to a single five-year term in office.

In the United Arab Emirates, the seven emirates each have their own ruler, but a Federal Supreme Council governs the country as a whole.

In Indonesia, the President is elected for a term of five years and can serve a maximum of two consecutive terms.

In Switzerland, the government is composed of a seven-member Federal Council, with each member serving as both a head of state and a head of a federal department.

In Nigeria, the President is limited to two terms in office, but the constitution was amended in 2018 to remove term limits for state governors and other elected officials.

In Egypt, the President is elected for a term of four years and can serve a maximum of two consecutive terms.

In Poland, the President is elected for a term of five years and can serve a maximum of two consecutive terms.

In Greece, the President is elected for a term of five years by the Parliament and cannot serve more than two terms.

In Ukraine, the President is elected for a term of five years and can serve a maximum of two consecutive terms.

In Peru, the President is elected for a term of five years and cannot serve consecutive terms.

In Colombia, the President is elected for a term of four years and cannot serve consecutive terms.

Printed in Great Britain
by Amazon

20065192R00068